Would You
Rather?
Easter
EDITION

Would You Rather?

Easter

EDITION

Hop into a Hilarious
Springtime Game for Kids

LINDSEY DALY

Z KIDS · NEW YORK

For Debbie and Susan,
thank you for believing in me.

Contents

Introduction

There are so many ways to enjoy Easter: dyeing eggs, watching or walking in an Easter parade, participating in an Easter egg hunt, or my personal favorite, stuffing your face with chocolate and candy from your Easter basket! Add a new tradition to your family's Easter celebration by playing a fun and insightful game of "Would You Rather?" Liven up Easter dinner or spring break road trips with hilarious and thought-provoking questions!

The questions in this book revolve around all aspects of Easter and are meant for kids ages 8–12 and their families. Each question is designed to make readers think critically about different situations and start funny, thoughtful, and creative conversations. You'll be amazed by what you can learn about somebody through their responses.

Would You Rather? Easter Edition is meant to be played as a game with winners for individual questions, chapters, and the entire book (though you can play it without keeping score, too). Since creativity and humor have no age, it's a level playing field for everyone. The main goal of these 160+ questions is to laugh and have fun with your family and friends by stretching your imagination and mind while convincing others that your answer is best.

Family, friends, and an interactive game of "Would You Rather" questions are the perfect recipe for a lively Easter celebration that no one will forget. So, grab "everybunny" you know and enjoy an "eggciting" game of "Would You Rather?" this Easter!

Rules of
the Game

Get a group of friends or family members together for an Easter game of wits and creativity. The more the merrier!

* The game is played in eight rounds with twenty questions in each round.

* Players rotate the responsibility of being the "judge" and read the question aloud to the group.

* Players will have one minute to develop their answer with an explanation.

* Players will take turns sharing their answers.

* The judge of that round will then select the answer that they enjoyed the most based on humor, creativity, or logic. The player whose answer was chosen will be awarded a point for that question.

* If only two people are playing, the judge (the player reading the question) assigns 1 to 5 points for the answer (5 being the best answer) and records it with the other player's name in the space provided below the question.

* When all players complete the round, tally up the points to determine the winner for that round.

* In the event of a tie at the end of a round, the two players who are tied will answer the tiebreaker question. All remaining players will vote on the best answer. If only two people are playing, whoever makes the other player laugh wins.

* When players complete the book, the winner of the most rounds is the champion!

ROUND

1

Here Comes the Easter Bunny!

Would you rather
have a fluffy cotton tail
or
floppy bunny ears?

WINNER: POINTS:

Would you rather
have two giant front
teeth like a bunny
or
giant feet?

WINNER: POINTS:

Would you rather
eat a spoonful of bunny pellets
or
a handful of hay?

WINNER: POINTS:

Would you rather
help the Easter Bunny hide eggs
or
oversee an Easter Egg Roll?

WINNER: POINTS:

Would you rather
snap a selfie with the
Easter Bunny
or
do the Bunny Hop dance
together?

WINNER: POINTS:

Would you rather
eat nothing but carrots
every day for a year
or
lettuce?

WINNER: POINTS:

Would you rather
have long whiskers
or
a bright pink nose?

WINNER: POINTS:

Would you rather
hop as quickly as a bunny
or
hear as clearly?

WINNER: POINTS:

Would you rather

have a nose that twitches every
time you smell something

or

have eyes on the sides
of your head?

WINNER: POINTS:

Would you rather

have soft bunny fur instead
of human hair

or

unusually sharp teeth?

WINNER: POINTS:

Would you rather
spend the day giving
out candy with the
Easter Bunny
or
one hour in his
enchanted forest?

WINNER: POINTS:

Would you rather
have the Easter Bunny as a pet
or
Santa as your best friend?

WINNER: POINTS:

Would you rather
compete against the Easter Bunny
in a game of hopscotch
or
jump rope?

WINNER: POINTS:

Would you rather
have the Easter Bunny's
head on your body
or
your head on the
Easter Bunny's body?

WINNER: POINTS:

Would you rather
visit the Easter Bunny's
enchanted forest
or
Santa's workshop?

WINNER: POINTS:

Would you rather
turn into the Easter
Bunny every Easter
or
for the rest of
your life?

WINNER: POINTS:

Would you rather
write a children's book about the
magic of the Easter Bunny
or
be the star of a play about him?

WINNER: POINTS:

Would you rather
have a yard full of
Easter bunnies
or
reindeer?

WINNER: POINTS:

Would you rather
discover that the Easter Bunny
forgot to visit your house
or
that he ran out of eggs for the
whole neighborhood?

WINNER: POINTS:

Would you rather
challenge the Easter Bunny
to a jumping contest
or
a foot race?

WINNER: POINTS:

Would you rather
receive only healthy snacks
from the Easter Bunny
or
expired candy?

WINNER: _____ POINTS: _____

WINNER: _____

TOTAL POINTS: _____

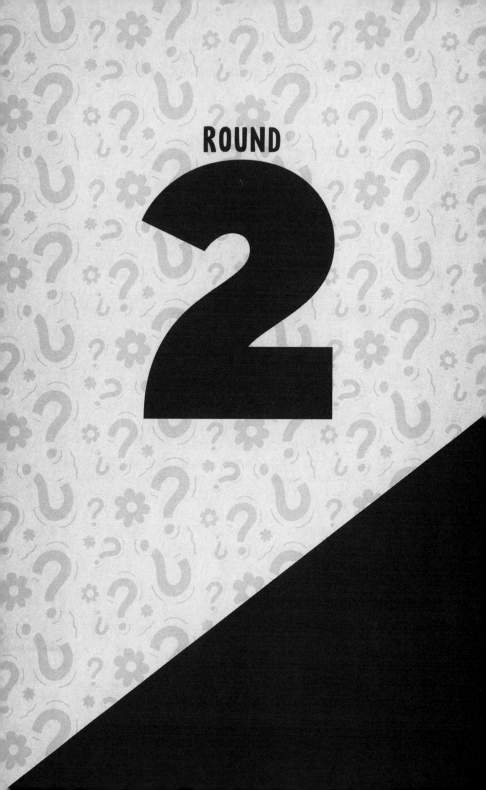

ROUND

2

Easter Eggs

Would you rather
hunt for Easter eggs in a swamp
or
a rain forest?

WINNER: POINTS:

Would you rather
dye real eggs
or
paint wooden ones?

WINNER: POINTS:

Would you rather
decorate your front lawn with
an Easter egg tree
or
a huge inflatable Easter Bunny?

WINNER: POINTS:

Would you rather
find a small prize in each
Easter egg at a hunt
or
receive a large prize for the
most eggs collected?

WINNER: POINTS:

Would you rather
hunt for eggs made
of chocolate
or
marshmallows?

WINNER: POINTS:

Would you rather
search for eggs the size
of pebbles in your lawn
or
one giant egg hidden
somewhere in your town?

WINNER: POINTS:

Would you rather
eat a raw egg every
day for a week
or
smell like hard-boiled
eggs for a month?

WINNER: POINTS:

Would you rather
drink a glass of vinegar
after dyeing eggs
or
red food coloring that stains
your lips and teeth?

WINNER: POINTS:

Would you rather
search for Easter eggs in
a lion's den
or
a bat cave?

WINNER: POINTS:

Would you rather
cook the eggs to be dyed
or
clean up when everyone
is finished dyeing?

WINNER: POINTS:

Would you rather
hunt for eggs on the
White House lawn
or
at the Statue of Liberty?

WINNER: POINTS:

Would you rather
open a plastic Easter egg
to find stale candy
or
an expired gift card?

WINNER: POINTS:

Would you rather
hunt for eggs in
a haunted house
or
a hall of mirrors?

WINNER: POINTS:

Would you rather
decorate eggs with spray paint
or
colorful chalk?

WINNER: POINTS:

Would you rather
take a bath in egg yolks
or
food coloring?

WINNER: POINTS:

Would you rather
search for eggs by yourself
or
with a team?

WINNER: POINTS:

Would you rather
hunt for Easter eggs in
the pouring rain
or
during a snowstorm?

WINNER: POINTS:

Would you rather
dye your Easter eggs all the
colors of the rainbow
or
paint them black and white
with special designs?

WINNER: POINTS:

Would you rather
find Easter eggs
filled with candy
or
money?

WINNER: POINTS:

Would you rather
walk through cobwebs to get
to the last Easter egg
or
a pricker bush?

WINNER: POINTS:

Would you rather

collect eggs in a basket with a
huge hole in the bottom

or

a metal shopping cart?

WINNER: _____   POINTS: _____

WINNER: _____

TOTAL POINTS: _____

ROUND

3

Candy All
Around!

Would you rather
take a chocolate shower
or
swim in a pool of jelly beans?

WINNER: POINTS:

Would you rather
sleep in a bed made of
Peeps marshmallows
or
cotton candy?

WINNER: POINTS:

Would you rather
be trapped inside a giant, hollow
chocolate bunny
or
a Cadbury Creme Egg?

WINNER: POINTS:

Would you rather
receive an Easter basket
full of sweet treats
or
sour candy?

WINNER: POINTS:

Would you rather
eat a chocolate-covered cricket
or
a slug dipped in
marshmallow sauce?

WINNER: POINTS:

Would you rather
bite into a Cadbury Creme Egg
that is filled with ketchup
or
hot sauce?

WINNER: POINTS:

Would you rather
give up sugar for
two months
or
TV?

WINNER: POINTS:

Would you rather
eat nothing but candy
every day for a year
or
go two years without it?

WINNER: POINTS:

Would you rather
have a chocolate fountain
in your bedroom
or
a gumball machine?

WINNER: POINTS:

Would you rather
enter the zombie apocalypse
with only jelly beans
or
Hershey's Kisses?

WINNER: POINTS:

Would you rather
brush your teeth with lollipops
or
floss with Nerds Rope?

WINNER: POINTS:

Would you rather
receive twenty of your
favorite candy bars
or
thirty different types
of candy?

WINNER: POINTS:

Would you rather
have a pet chicken that
lays chocolate eggs
or
marshmallows?

WINNER: POINTS:

Would you rather
eat a chocolate bunny filled
with peanut butter
or
Rice Krispies?

WINNER: POINTS:

Would you rather
live in a house made
of chewy candy
or
hard candy?

WINNER: POINTS:

Would you rather
have a Peeps marshmallow
as a pet
or
a chocolate bunny?

WINNER: POINTS:

Would you rather
have to share all your Easter candy
with your least favorite classmate
or
throw it all away?

WINNER: POINTS:

Would you rather
eat a jelly bean that
someone sneezed on
or
that fell in mud?

WINNER: POINTS:

Would you rather
be caught in a rainstorm
of pastel M&M's
or
Sour Patch Kids?

WINNER: POINTS:

Would you rather
eat 100 chocolate eggs
in one sitting
or
100 pieces of licorice?

WINNER: POINTS:

Would you rather
eat a chocolate egg filled
with dead bugs
or
bunny poop?

WINNER: POINTS:

WINNER: _____

TOTAL POINTS: _____

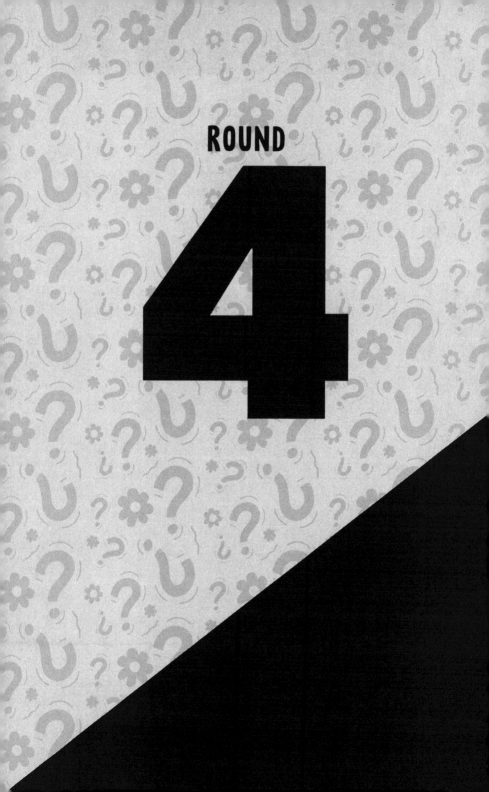

ROUND

4

Easter Basket Bonanza

Would you rather
get an Easter basket
full of books
or
video games?

WINNER: POINTS:

Would you rather
complete a physical challenge in
order to find your Easter basket
or
solve logic puzzles?

WINNER: POINTS:

Would you rather
have Easter grass as hair
or
eyelashes?

WINNER: POINTS:

Would you rather
find a garden snake in your
Easter basket
or
a thick layer of mold?

WINNER: POINTS:

Would you rather
make a list of items that you
want in your Easter basket
or
be surprised?

WINNER: POINTS:

Would you rather
receive an Easter basket
filled with healthy snacks
or
candies that you've
never heard of?

WINNER: POINTS:

Would you rather
get an Easter basket that's
been infested with ants
or
full of cobwebs?

WINNER: POINTS:

Would you rather
sleep on a bed made of
Easter basket plastic
or
bamboo?

WINNER: POINTS:

Would you rather
wear an empty Easter basket
as a hat for two weeks
or
as shoes?

WINNER: POINTS:

Would you rather
receive an Easter basket
full of art supplies
or
board games?

WINNER: POINTS:

Would you rather
find rotten eggs in your
Easter basket
or
moldy candy?

WINNER: POINTS:

Would you rather
make custom Easter
baskets for a living
or
design Easter decorations?

WINNER: POINTS:

Would you rather
receive a small basket of gifts every
week for a month in the spring
or
a large one on Easter?

WINNER: POINTS:

Would you rather
find a live chick in your
Easter basket
or
a bunny?

WINNER: POINTS:

Would you rather
receive an Easter basket with
accessories for your phone
or
a new gaming system?

WINNER: POINTS:

Would you rather
get an Easter basket
lined with hay
or
seaweed?

WINNER: POINTS:

Would you rather
make an Easter basket out of clay
or
papier-mâché?

WINNER: POINTS:

Would you rather
wear a shirt made of Easter
basket cellophane wrap
or
ribbon?

WINNER: POINTS:

Would you rather
use an Easter basket as your
school bag for an entire year
or
as a travel bag once for vacation?

WINNER: POINTS:

Would you rather
receive an Easter basket full
of hard-boiled eggs
or
pickles?

WINNER: POINTS:

Would you rather

discover a cockroach at the
bottom of your Easter basket
or
a family of spiders?

WINNER: POINTS:

WINNER: _____

TOTAL POINTS: _____

ROUND

5

Easter Feast

Would you rather
eat undercooked ham
or
overcooked lamb chops?

WINNER: POINTS:

Would you rather
have a slice of an Easter cake
with uncooked batter in it
or
eggshells?

WINNER: POINTS:

Would you rather
have a stomachache
during Easter dinner
or
a toothache?

WINNER: POINTS:

Would you rather
eat ten hot cross buns
or
twenty chocolate eggs?

WINNER: POINTS:

Would you rather
be responsible for preparing
the ham for your entire family
or
dessert?

WINNER: POINTS:

Would you rather
eat a chocolate-covered carrot
or
a bag of carrot-flavored
jelly beans?

WINNER: POINTS:

Would you rather
have an Easter feast of
rabbit pellets
or
birdseed?

WINNER: POINTS:

Would you rather
eat raw cake batter
or
burnt cookies?

WINNER: POINTS:

Would you rather
eat Easter dinner with no utensils
or
using only knives?

WINNER: POINTS:

Would you rather
compete in a family bake-off
or
a pie-eating contest?

WINNER: POINTS:

Would you rather
eat lamb chops that have been
sitting out for a week
or
mashed potatoes?

WINNER: POINTS:

Would you rather
have Easter dinner by yourself
or
prepare a meal for 50 people?

WINNER: POINTS:

Would you rather
sit at the kids' table with
a screaming toddler
or
the adults' table with
boring conversations?

WINNER: POINTS:

Would you rather
eat a deviled egg-flavored cake pop
or
a ham-flavored cookie?

WINNER: POINTS:

Would you rather
eat dessert for the main course
or
the main course for dessert?

WINNER: POINTS:

Would you rather
eat cold pork chops
or
hot egg salad?

WINNER: POINTS:

Would you rather
eat Easter bread made with salt
or
roast chicken seasoned with
powdered sugar?

WINNER: POINTS:

Would you rather
take a bath in carrot juice
or
melted Hershey's Kisses?

WINNER: POINTS:

Would you rather

eat a casserole that a guest
stuck their fingers in

or

green beans that fell on the floor?

WINNER: POINTS:

Would you rather

eat burnt hot cross buns

or

marshmallows?

WINNER: POINTS:

Would you rather
have Easter dinner at
a fancy restaurant
or
at home?

WINNER: POINTS:

WINNER: _____

TOTAL POINTS: _____

ROUND

6

The Easter Bunny's Friends

Would you rather
have a pet duck that
quacks nonstop
or
a pet rooster that wakes you
up early every morning
with loud crowing?

WINNER: POINTS:

Would you rather
have a chick hide eggs
for the Easter Bunny
or
a fox?

WINNER: POINTS:

Would you rather
have sheep's wool for
skin for two months
or
"bah" uncontrollably for two weeks?

WINNER: POINTS:

Would you rather
raise a fawn
or
a calf?

WINNER: POINTS:

Would you rather
watch baby chicks hatch
from their eggs
or
a butterfly emerge
from its chrysalis?

WINNER: POINTS:

Would you rather
protect baby bunnies in a rabbit
burrow from predators
or
a nest of robin eggs?

WINNER: POINTS:

Would you rather
be a sheepherder
or
a dairy farmer?

WINNER: POINTS:

Would you rather
run a petting zoo
or
volunteer at a bunny sanctuary?

WINNER: POINTS:

Would you rather
go mountain climbing
with a goat
or
race a rabbit?

WINNER: POINTS:

Would you rather
have a duck bill for a mouth
or
a chicken beak?

WINNER: POINTS:

Would you rather
make a quacking sound
every time you laugh
or
a bleating sound?

WINNER: POINTS:

Would you rather
be chased by a
gaggle of geese
or
a flock of sheep?

WINNER: POINTS:

Would you rather
spend the night in
a chicken coop
or
a rabbit hutch?

WINNER: POINTS:

Would you rather
cluck like a chicken
every time you sneeze
or
buzz like a bee?

WINNER: POINTS:

Would you rather
find a litter of bunnies
in your basement
or
stray puppies?

WINNER: POINTS:

Would you rather
have a cottontail like a bunny
or
short legs like a chick?

WINNER: POINTS:

Would you rather
have the ability to
speak to ducks
or
lambs?

WINNER: POINTS:

Would you rather
be friends with the
Easter Bunny
or
Bugs Bunny?

WINNER: POINTS:

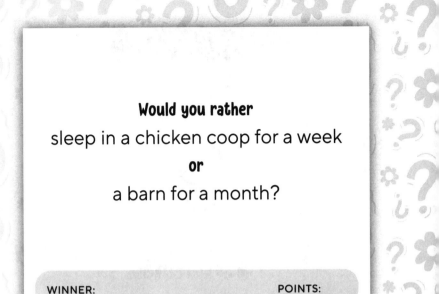

Would you rather
sleep in a chicken coop for a week
or
a barn for a month?

WINNER: POINTS:

Would you rather
try to catch a chicken
or
a rabbit?

WINNER: POINTS:

Would you rather
be the size of a
duckling for a day
or
a horse?

WINNER: POINTS:

WINNER

ROUND 6

WINNER: _____

TOTAL POINTS: _____

ROUND

7

Spring Has Sprung

Would you rather
Easter be permanently
moved to winter
or
summer?

WINNER: POINTS:

Would you rather
sneeze nonstop during
a beautiful spring
or
feel fine in a rainy spring?

WINNER: POINTS:

Would you rather
fly on the back of
a giant robin
or
butterfly?

WINNER: POINTS:

Would you rather
find a pot of gold at the
end of a rainbow
or
lottery tickets?

WINNER: POINTS:

Would you rather
grow a garden full
of beautiful flowers
or
fresh vegetables?

WINNER: POINTS:

Would you rather
turn your backyard into
a butterfly conservatory
or
bird aviary?

WINNER: POINTS:

Would you rather

watch a spring training baseball
game in the pouring rain

or

snow?

WINNER: POINTS:

Would you rather

have your picture taken
at a flower farm

or

in front of a rainbow?

WINNER: POINTS:

Would you rather
be a bumblebee
for a week
or
a bird?

WINNER: POINTS:

Would you rather
have a picnic in a botanical garden
or
a meadow?

WINNER: POINTS:

Would you rather
write a poem about
Mother Nature
or
Easter traditions?

WINNER: POINTS:

Would you rather
get caught on your bicycle
during a thunderstorm
or
a flash flood?

WINNER: POINTS:

Would you rather
be a sunflower
or
a tulip?

WINNER: POINTS:

Would you rather
get stung by a bee
or
a rash from poison ivy?

WINNER: POINTS:

Would you rather

have all your classes outside
during spring

or

take one special field trip?

WINNER: POINTS:

Would you rather

grow a plant that doesn't
require any water

or

sunlight?

WINNER: POINTS:

Would you rather
have drizzle every day
or
thunderstorms three
times a week?

WINNER: POINTS:

Would you rather
play an April Fool's joke
on your parents
or
your teachers?

WINNER: POINTS:

Would you rather
go hiking during a rainstorm
or
high humidity?

WINNER: POINTS:

Would you rather
experience a spring that
is unusually hot
or
unusually cold?

WINNER: POINTS:

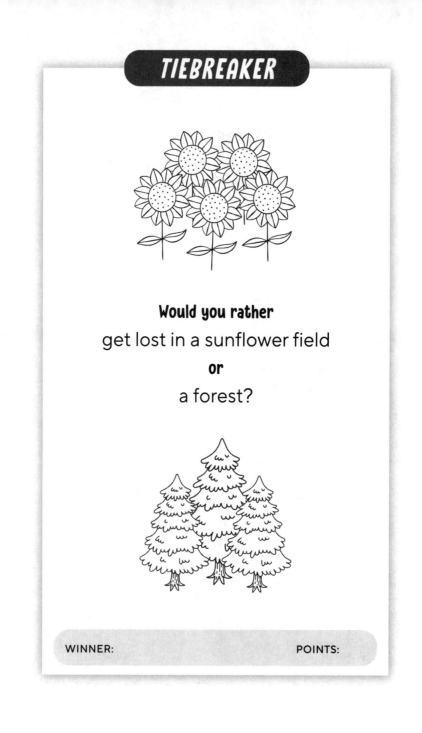

Would you rather

get lost in a sunflower field

or

a forest?

WINNER: POINTS:

WINNER

ROUND 7

WINNER: _____

TOTAL POINTS: _____

ROUND

8

Easter Traditions

Would you rather
lead the Easter parade wearing
a bath towel
or
walk in the middle wearing
fancy clothes?

WINNER: POINTS:

Would you rather
have the funniest
Easter bonnet
or
the most stylish?

WINNER: POINTS:

Would you rather
have a long spring break and
short summer vacation
or
no spring break and a superlong
summer vacation?

WINNER: POINTS:

Would you rather
roll a raw Easter egg
or
a wooden one?

WINNER: POINTS:

Would you rather
attend an Easter
service at dawn
or
midnight?

Would you rather
attend the White House
Egg Roll in your winter coat
or
bathing suit?

Would you rather
have the most athletic people on
your Easter egg relay race team
or
the most strategic?

WINNER: POINTS:

Would you rather
revise classic Easter traditions
or
create your own?

WINNER: POINTS:

Would you rather

wake up early to get a head start
on the Easter egg hunt

or

sleep in and collect whatever is left?

WINNER: POINTS:

Would you rather

have the Easter Bunny hide
the eggs in your house

or

outside?

WINNER: POINTS:

Would you rather
wear an Easter bonnet for
your school picture
or
to school every day for a month?

WINNER: POINTS:

Would you rather
compete in an egg relay race
in your best Easter clothes
or
go to Easter services
in your pajamas?

WINNER: POINTS:

Would you rather
trip someone in the
Easter parade by accident
or
sprain your ankle?

WINNER: POINTS:

Would you rather
participate in the Polish tradition
of "blessing of the baskets"
or
give the Easter lily to
someone special?

WINNER: POINTS:

Would you rather

spend Easter in another country
learning new traditions

or

host someone at your home
to teach them yours?

WINNER: POINTS:

Would you rather

fall in the mud in your Easter clothes

or

have your pants split open
during Easter services?

WINNER: POINTS:

Would you rather
direct an Easter play
or
be the star of one?

WINNER: POINTS:

Would you rather
make your Easter bonnet
out of recycled clothing
or
old Christmas decorations?

WINNER: POINTS:

Would you rather
bake cookies with your family
in preparation for Easter
or
a bunny cake?

WINNER: POINTS:

Would you rather
celebrate Easter traditions
that you know
or
learn new ones?

WINNER: POINTS:

Would you rather
go 40 days of Lent
without your phone
or
computer?

WINNER: POINTS:

WINNER: _____

TOTAL POINTS: _____

This certificate
is awarded to

_____

for being blissfully brilliant,
incredibly insightful, and
curiously creative!

Even the Easter Bunny is
impressed!

CONGRATULATIONS!

About the Author

 Lindsey Daly grew up in Andover, New Jersey. She graduated from Ramapo College of New Jersey with a BA in history and a certification in secondary education. Lindsey is a middle school social studies teacher and the author of the best-selling Would You Rather? series. She lives with her dog, Teddy, in New Jersey.

Parents, for more information about Lindsey and her books, follow her online:

 @lindseydalybooks

🐦 @LindseyDaly10

Hi, parents and caregivers,

We hope your child enjoyed *Would You Rather? Easter Edition*. If you have any questions or concerns about this book, or have received a damaged copy, please contact customerservice@penguinrandomhouse.com. We're here and happy to help. Also, please consider writing a review on your favorite retailer's website to let others know what you and your child thought of the book!

Sincerely,
The Zeitgeist Team